apricot

Katie O'Pray

Out-Spoken Press
London

Published by Out-Spoken Press,
Unit 39, Containerville
1 Emma Street
London, E2 9FP

A CIP record for this title is available from the British Library.

First edition published 2022
ISBN: 978-1-7399021-0-0

Typeset in Adobe Caslon
Design by Patricia Ferguson
Printed and bound by Print Resources

Out-Spoken Press is supported using public funding by the National Lottery through Arts Council England.
Contact: press@outspokenldn.com

For my families – inherited and chosen

Contents

IV. WHERE DO YOU THINK YOU WILL SURVIVE?

PLEASE HAND OVER THE NAMES
YOU ANSWER MOST FAITHFULLY TO

tomcat

i don't look enough like the tubby girl
in my own ID photo / with my compressed
bones now / my jaw / a set square / the tomcat
curled up in my throat

closed windows have been steaming
my lungs / 2 dumplings changing texture
under my jumper / mina says my voice
is lower than when she met me

I love the sound my chest makes when I cough

when last sunday my dad / took clippers to my hair
in the kitchen / sacred buzz softer than   .
the barber's / chuckling behind his ready-readers
like the forgivable man / he has ripened into

my gender falling in clumps / we remembered
how to hug each other still / even
with my body / more boisterous
than it's ever been / half the son   .
he hasn't clocked he's got

insulin-dependent

there's hard work in keeping a body faulty.
so little honour in all the sums required

to swallow a sandwich, fed up on needles, the reasons
these muscles twitch. it's tedious to go on

answering, numerically, what should be
in the blood, in the sauce of baked beans,

the split doses trickling into lame tissue, quietly, excelling
at masking all my clots & cannulas. here I am, faultily

vomiting at barbecues. at the mercy
of rum punch & deep pan pizza. my shy belly

speckled over with jabs — relentless
tally of days.

OUTPATIENT

    I often come-to inside a person who
is sitting on a wet bench / shivering
& creating a smell / hiding their cheeks
from cyclists

    a kind-throated woman
will try her best to catch their eye / their legs
are matchsticks / sparking against
the damp wood & she is asking
if they are sure / they're okay

I'm not sure
how much
of me
is here

which self
is moving
my jaw

which name
this anatomy
answers to

a chill last night
just waking
in tights
thick socks
more trousers
more trousers

I might be hypomanic again
MY HEAD IS FULL

sweating something out
house key under my pillow
under the toilet-seat the crystallised
sugar & toxins
the unjailed unjust faces
I've been keeping
in my contacts

      a sad ugly number
I have gained
      now I'm large
-ly happy & almost dead

hungry glitch

so I'm in big tesco
considering nimble bread & polos
the panny announcements
the parentless child

in my furtive dreams   ungodly
I would snatch
a whole trifle — a frenzy
of sliced cheese & doughnuts
a hungry glitch
with custard

on my way out
I will force my mouth down stern
for the woman at the tobacco counter
to eyeball slow against my photo
she won't ask how I got like this
my face all out of shape
I don't think my school teachers
would recognise me now
white knuckling a large sweet potato

devastating

sharp elbows   all of me   ankles
eating so much spinach   soon my body
will be an undesirable shiv
some days   I want my pain

to be the loudest thing in a room   to be devastating
more pungent than I could explain   a waste
of so much medicine   gone   visibly foul

I'll keep on wearing
these afflictions like a habit

for as long as there are men
that I keep dreaming of cremated
or heavy-footed across the pews
of my sleep

carrying my unheavy coffin
and having to live
the rest of their lives
with those hands

lemon

sitting in the kitchen
I am scratching off the rind with my fingernails
strands of waxy yellow collecting on the table
spun gold and duckling feathers
until the pith is stark naked
a chalky sponge cradling the fruit inside
I am patently tearing it off
layers of supple cotton in my hands
strings of white tissue weaving through my fingers
winding tighter
binding me at the knuckles
my dad is appearing in the dusk of the doorway
somewhere fruit falls from bare branches
I never realised lemons grew best in late winter
but they must because this is what he is telling me
as he unravels the pithy ropes from my wrists
he closes his fingers around them like calloused bracelets
gauging how loose they fit
shocked by how empty his hands are
now I'm taking a segment from the undressed lemon on the
table
pretending I'm not terrified of piercing the lucent skin
of letting the sharp juice bleed out
it scathes my tongue with such a bite
I almost don't feel guilty chewing it

WHO WAS THERE
WHEN THE WORST WAS
HAPPENING?

WHO WOULD COME
IF WE PHONED & ASKED?

[*Simon*]

when I say *today is a hard day*   I mean it's only 11
& I've already cried off my makeup over-eating
an underripe banana   a handful of walnuts
& my jeans are even bigger than they were
last night   when I say *I'll see you*
in a bit   I mean the puddles are glassed
over & my legs near buckling but my hands
are too big for a handful of raisins
to be small enough I mean I'm not small
enough   when I say *I'm feeling*
down today   I mean there's too much
to start unpacking & what would speech
unscar anyway   & then I say:
I hate it here   which means   here
in myself   in this blunt world
not in your dressing gown   where I am
waiting for you   to surprise me

[*Scarlett; Luke; Dylan; Adam*]

IV.
She is unlooping
my hair from itself, thighs
bowing under my head,
there's a man who fathered an alien she says,
she says *they called him starseed,*
we are wearing down the evening, steady burn on a wick
and paddling in the halflight, I can't stop
talking because she does not know me, no image
to disrupt, the high
falls and I am putting on my coat, she says
wait
turns her mouth up into mine

III.
The girls in the garden with us are singing
and telling their boyfriends they want
to fuck, the nighttime
cooling my sunburn
through my sleeves, the fruit
punch is all rum, the picnic blanket dappled
with cherry burns, I don't remember
the lips, just that they happened
just the glowsticks, the singing —
the places where all the veins meet

II.
French sunlight
slapping the back of the bus, teachers dozing
in the front row, I am sucking

on a peppermint, my hatching teeth,
sticky suede seat, he is
lean lipped and freckled, sloppy tongued
but enthusiastic and if we don't do it now,
what will we hang on the fridge!

I.
There is damp sand pushed under my fingernails,
I am squatting, soft legged over some painted
wooden blocks, white knee socks
on the hopscotch corner of the playground
only watched by a ceramic frog, sickly
belly and I don't even think
he says anything, I've never tasted
someone else's spit but girls
are silent in the swallow
and his dad calls me sweetheart over the gate

[Q]

I spend most of my days thirsty, holed
up in my eyelids, trying to get warmer.

I am probably going to die soon
or young, at least, the pamphlets say.

there's no double meaning to this one.
not a punchline or a snare.

it's statistical, unfortunate. I'm waiting
under empty wrappers, for you, greasy brown

paper bags, laughing. thinking: well
I could go on bedbound, and you, well

-intentioned, tying my knots
like pretzels. buttering my crumpets.

let me teach you my favourite trick
where I draw in a whole box
of cereal and the sugar draws all
the water out of my body.

watch me pass the untouched calories
on to your stained toilet bowl. my fat
tissue perfecting its escapology.

want to see me do it again?
biscuits this time. do you wonder

how I've been keeping so frail
with all of this potato
gone wet in my mouth?

I confess: it's my faulty organs
turned shortcut — the best I can do
with sleight of body —
the wicked privilege of choice.

[*Eloise*]

    I ate toast with the girl
before she was obituated, let her plait my hair, her front teeth
denting her bottom lip, daytime TV, the girl still

    a girl when she tapped out
of this world at the barrier, riding a child's
fare, she split open the tube map and found
an exit, wound her ending
body around a carriage like string noosed around a finger —

    a method I learnt for memory recall — everyone has,
at least once, felt the brutality
of calendars — their indifferent turning
of pages — a sharp tug on a string on a finger brings pain,
movement, twitching back into grey matter

    I am trying so hard
not to forget Eloise, and I understand why
I didn't ask who found her, whose intrinsic muscles
were plucked at by her face

    didn't want to know
which stop she ended the trip at, call me selfish, I don't
want to know when I'm passing through her deathbed. her dad
seemed so collected in the debris, I didn't want to imagine
him crumpled, trackside, saying *yes,*
that's her, or it was this time yesterday.

18

[a girl], before

moon in leo! I am squealing at you
after you find out what time you were born
and I've scrutinised your natal chart
we're very idealistic
a man scoffs too wetly at this
and too close to my ear
garbles something about the planets and a drunk girl
I can't remember why he's in your living room with us
pulling the early hours around our fingers like chewing gum
in the creases in the leather couch
his pupils are saucers of oil
I can remember the untying of the evening
the wind hurling itself at your brackish windows
and the emptying of bottles
there is a stained armchair in the doorway
that he, this man, has carried here from a few streets away
I don't pay attention at this point
to the strength he must have in his arms
I am small in the middle of the basement
his hand pressing on one of my thighs and yours on the other
I've known this man for bleary hours
you since childhood
but tonight the two of you are wearing the same face
looking at my mouth with the same dampening want
you will do something horrible after this moment
you'll mutate in front of me
it'll be months before I let myself unfold the impact
but right now you are listening to me ramble
I don't know yet what shape my throat makes
in the clamp of your grip
people who assault people are still theoretical

how could I be afraid of someone who sounds
so much like me
you and I used to play the piano together
and here the man is showing us photos
of his gap-toothed baby
he's someone's dad and foolishly
I am planning on waking up unchanged
crooked and pink with the warmth of us
seeing each other just the same
in the daylight

[*CJ*]

       shot of you curled over my ankle
tongue poking out
biro and safety pin
you are making a mark on me forever
we're in one of those tv shows
where the teenagers go off the rails but never die there
you've hacked your hair in this scene you are clearly
Going Through Something
and I am on top of a multi-storey car park with you
pointing down at a basketball court
it's a matchbox from up here
the boys between the bars are our age
waiting to be rubbed the wrong way
and torn into flame
and I know we're both thinking
about how much damage we could do
but those are not our lines
it's too sooty a storyline
to be wrapped up in 40 minutes
cider cans and our lips on each other's mouths are more
appealing to our audience
       shot of us outside a bar
this scene probably won't get used
too many screens of smoke and grown men
slurring and jostling, casting shadows
we are nostalgic for childhood without realising
that we are still holding it
we are denouncing misogyny and capitalism between
coughs

we are an entire solar system
      cut to us laying in a loft conversion
morrissey is playing on vinyl but the needle keeps skipping

[*John*]

I can boil his limescale   I can look like I need him
to pop the lids off my pickle jars   silly me! in mornings
trying to chew yoghurt   off a teaspoon   watching him
hold all my ribs   or   both my lovely shoulders
in the mirror

we devote whole weekdays   to replicating the smoke
in the carpets   drinking my spilt water off his lap
I promise   I am helpless

predictable as monday   until his touch strays where
I had told it not to   silly me!   disappointingly
undeniable   until I take my chance to call it   carrying
out my shoes

I've got to flex my ribcage   now   fill up
my own bins   for a while   look
at him — so sorry
on my doorstep   offering ingestible
chemicals   3 handwritten letters
of apology   & pleas of expensive
blueberries

[*ivy*]

it's a shame / I want you / and me / grilling bread
cold off the tiles of your mum's kitchen / the volume of trains
periodically shattering the windows / it's embarrassing
to want / your mum's fickle lack of toaster / or my mum's
expensive carbohydrates / chewed out / pathetic
to want you / again / on that lawn / making the birches
feel young / sunflowers taller than the fence
your freckled shoulders higher than my dad's / don't you
want that kind of young we were / in those names
that are long since buried / in my wide jeans / that we'd have
so much room in now / it's a shame / I'm really
a schoolgirl / grown up / on your coattails / doodling us
the scandalous press of your palm / across my mouth

[*Katie*]

But I want to stay slimlined & electric
anorexic beauty   eclectic
with my teeth   defying gravity
with those legs   I'm so feeble
you can see it   thru my sweatshirt
people are understanding
my hairline fractures
untouchable
by my own proud doing
bones diagnoseably brittle   now
the fear of breaking them
is infectious   I am cautious
in the kitchen   clean-mouthed
kissing the calories off
my boyfriend's chest

IS YOUR ILLNESS OLD ENOUGH
TO HOLD A SENTENCE?

TO DRINK
FROM A BEAKER?

in june — the doctors write with bad news —
I don't think the pain is muscular — I think the
binder will be having an effect
on your posture — your perception — & ability to breathe &
stand up straight
because of the weight — the density – the lack
thereof — because of the pain & aerated marrow —
the obvious
malnutrition — you have performed — we expected
the alkaline in your blood vessels – the way your ribs
often crack on windowsills — we can see your lungs trying —
lighting up
in the results — your waning bones — scanned
flat as a piece of paper

it's november & — the doctors write — o
　　your deranged liver — humorous clavicle —
　　　　are you feeling frightened of them?

by february — there
will be a review — amongst a body
of professionals — it might be best you don't attend — given
the uncertainty — you are reasonably compliant — as the
dietitian
notes — you are of soundish
mind — but the likelihood that you will — drop — down —
dead
is statistically high — we are simply concerned
you won't make it through the weekend — we are simply
surprised
to see you — standing — we are
being explicitly dutiful — lawfully caring — you can see
we've put all of this in writing

in cambridge, I think *no one is that thin
without trying.*

I think I am the only alien not using
my allotted condiments, no noted
yoghurt preference.

I am the only one of the patients not
deficient in calcium. I walk with a hunch,

anyway. the posture of an apology.
at the concourse, the owner
of the therapy dog asks me which ward
I'm dubbing *home.* tells me I look well
for it. each night, my bicep fills
the adult cuff. my blood pressure:
unremarkable.

in the real world   it's easy to be worrying
to keep a hungry waist   and prove really how little
a person can become   there's nothing special
about being thin here every   body's sick
in a hospital

we do our crochet   in armchairs   get taught
how to stretch   how to sit down
over and over   to our 2 rich tea biscuits and 2 small
satsumas   how to pronounce '*I need*'

after ward round — the doctors relay — clean plates
are an expectation & your frail heart — when you
stand — is alarming — we've noted — how your elbows stir
at night — hourly — in the torchlight — the team can see
how hard this is — this week
we grant you — fresh air — watercolours & clay — clear
medicines that fizz in a row like spirits — think about harm
reduction — which care pathway beckons — you can stay
here as long as you need

on both the night & day shift   the nurses
have become hardened   to the horrors   we spell out
so laboriously with our skeletons   our muted jumping
jacks   the clogged drains we splash about in   the childish
acts of our   made-childish bodies   twice weekly   poker
-faced   they write down our measurements   the bleak
flesh we indulge in   & catch us out
when they look up from the numbers to ask:
is there anything else you have to say

inside   summer's over
and I'm still so far away
haven't been through
my own front door
in months
haven't paced
in anyone's kitchen

instead I'm sitting in an armchair
watching a TV rippling
from inside a sealed cabinet
nursing a full stomach and the kind of memory
that pops ajar like a fridge

in jeans   a woman
with a masters has been teaching me
how to make friendship bracelets
I have to keep braiding them longer
to fit around our swelling wrists

there is unspoken law here
forbidding mention
of how we've all been looking fuller

in the bathrooms — we have tiny bendy mirrors
I ask of them: is a body still a body
when it doesn't recognise itself
when it stops fitting its favourite trousers

in session
the psychologist says:
this time, after you leave us
how will you tell people
when you aren't okay

and I've been in here since beetroot season
should be home by marrow

if I keep scraping the yoghurt from the pot
and talking about the flashbacks
of greedy hands
the size of the cereal box
the quiet things that make us
look the way we do

I listen to thin women advise each other
on how best to eat kitkats and do other good
things with their lips
I want to feel intact

on re-admission to the real world — the doctors write —
together — we've interrupted the dying — mitigated
the illness — which you found — simultaneously
empowering & calorific — acknowledging a degree
of ambivalence — unforeseen
luck — a series of collaborative meals — you want to be
home — more than you want to be
thin — despite complex — intense & changeable
maladies — reluctance — you have restored
some body — we admire your decision — that
you've made one — we've made no adjustments
to the contingency plans — we can only give you
your last hot lunch — the first week's worth
of medication — for risk of relapse — as always —
we'll put HIGH — though we are hopeful
we won't be seeing you again

WHERE
DO YOU THINK YOU WILL
SURVIVE?

in your kitchen

one of us kneeling at the oven door
we're baking our own wedding cake
your hands on the wet cutlery   ginger
shedding into a mixing bowl I trust
my gut   your dancer's fingers always
quick stepping at my pelvis   half moon
-walking down my apron   touch
starved like we are practicing worship
functional love godly
domesticity

I tell you where it's not *hurting*   but it is
tender & which parts of me are overdue
for a firmer elbow   your upper lip
smudged from all the oil we've been
cooking with   we barely weigh
a thing   in our hats

with wide brims   you can't kiss
my face   we can't look up   beloved
there's no need
there isn't anything higher

in the train station

I snapped hard at mina   eyes   bugging   pranging   bigger
than my breasts   in the crook of the sunrise   frozen
tonsils ringing outwards   earlier   after this dark had come
I had eaten my dinner   in front of her   a neat tub
of chocolate ice cream   on the floor   in front of her
mirror

*

no man had dared   press up into me   that night in
the dancehall   my clavicle   a bad omen
lit up in neon   my hands   fire
-arms   poised at the temples   of the un-gentle
-men   taking their turns to brush up   against mina's
hairpiece
me   waiting in case she needs   my body   thrown
in front of her   body

*

brilliant pale & mantic   outside the bevy
where not one man   had defied or defiled my own
body's   chosen   ugly   its careful foreboding   admitting
they would not trust   themselves with me
a smoking cannon   if only
apparent by this one's fingers busied in his pockets
& his mate's fist   tightening round the neck
of his bottle   still
I had to go on explaining   that I don't sleep
soundly   in anybody's bed

*

years later   when mina is older & braver
than I was truly then   she tells me
how worried   she had been for me
that dawn   getting-home-safe
with shrapnel   in my mouth   fleeing heaven
hot   on the heels of daylight
& all the businessmen: slotting keenly
into my route like knives

under branches

I want to eat the sky today.
broad door of it open, pouring
sunlight onto an orchard. an easy blue
cheesecloth over the world.

on the good days

I am awake before I open my eyes,
knowing exactly where I am,
and the scales are whistling good morning.
I do not greet them.
the mirror in the hallway
is only bending light.
I fold hats out of the letters
that have been stiffening
on the table. the cupboards
halfway full and breakfast
is whatever I feel like.
I feel like cereal.
my stomach does not confuse itself
with desert or flood plain.
I am not counting steps
from the kitchen to the bathroom
and back. contrary to myself,
I'm mopping honeydew off my chin
with tissue and not waiting
for anything to pass.
the cornflakes in my bowl
are softening with milk;
simpler than the ways I can be
lessened, than the space around
my body.

in the dream

I finally lift the baby   above my head
he is gurgling   bald
& still a baby   his arms & legs limp
with awe   I haven't missed or dropped
a thing
        in the dream   I can't wear my fingers
around my own biceps like armbands
   I'm too old for it
I take the baby swimming
&   his legs are a fluke   he is floating
on instinct   I am paternally killing
mosquitos   we make no splash at all
        in the morning   I bite
into a whole apple   don't dirty
any knives or lipsticks
I put the toothbrush in my pink
mouth   breathe rectangles around
the mirror   my face
is a circle I don't know
the circumference of
blank & rested & waxing
towards fullness   all of my face
not pulled in towards my mouth
anymore   when I pull the baby

up out of his crib

he weighs less than I have gained

& he is almost not a baby

I lift him above my head

on the grass

I tell you *I do*
want to get better
this time & you go:
say it   with your chest
but I mean
if I am not striving
to overtake myself   as a cease
-lessly smaller thing if I'm not death
-defying & marvellous   what have I got
leftover   where would the proof
of harm be

in fullness

all my winters are happening on top of each other.
come june — emma & I will keep to our dinner
date. table enough for her bleached hair, my sunflower
spread & both of our more forgivable
illnesses.

last year inside the hospital,
she had told me apples
get their calories from sunlight.
churning it under the skin and who
can tally that? all the warmth

an apple learns, a crispened
beam, a glow turned
mouthful. what guilt is there
in fullness that started out
so bright?

on the bus

what strangers noticed first
was once my seasoned
thinness. how my head

had got too narrow for my face
and my knees too wide for both
my legs.

it was clear what I had done
to me.

all that pity
was very bad for my bones.

what's marvellous this morning
are my straight vertebrae,

the good deeds ringing silver
in my pockets, my attention
to healthy detail.

I'm at peace with the blonded charm
of a fleshed-out body,
jangling & trapping the sunlight —

the endless other things
I am capable of;
other things I am.

back home

I was a concerning rendition of youth   a calamity
of a child   & dizzying onwards into age & over
it   laying down in snow suddenly   I was twenty-two
perhaps   less capacitous than ever   reportedly
repeatedly leaving   hospitals   that year   waiting for
taxis in my flapping gown   my bruised veins
didn't want to be there   anymore   it didn't make me
interesting

by this autumn   there was nothing left
to prove   I'd had a big life on the outside
in bathrooms more porcelain than plastic
where I was trusted with my own bleach
& nobody had lunch with me
for a pay-check

I'd tried staying weak enough to lie down
all day long   willing any of my organs
to call time on us

but reluctant as winter   I conceded
got itchy in my cold bones   curious
about the news   & the price of scratchcards
milk   embarrassingly human
ways of participating in the world

I came out of the sickness
like a sore loser
saying: *okay   I'm ready   I'll bite*

Acknowledgements

To Mum, Dad, Daisy, Charlotte and Rob, as well as the wider family, for the love you give so fiercely to me; for your strength when it's been scary and sad; for all the things you've helped me be. To Henry, for who I am to him; for what he means to me.

To Tasha, Mina & Luke; for your infallible friendship, for staying the course, for being the siblings that choose me again and again.

To Charlotte Shevchenko Knight, Ollie O'Neill, Ella Sadie Guthrie and the endless other incredible people I've had the pleasure of meeting through poetry. To all of DEVOTION club, for revolutionising my writing practice and cultivating a space to which I can belong.

To *Magma Poetry*, *Bath Magg*, Words by the Water, Tracey Lingwood, East London NHS Foundation Trust's 'Break the Stigma' campaign, Bedfringe, Trickstar radio, The ruth weiss Foundation, Oxford Brookes Poetry and the University of Hertfordshire – all of whom have given homes to my poems and meaningful support for my writing.

To Dr Nick Hawkes, Claire Springall and the countless other professionals who go above and beyond for their patients, in an underfunded and problematic system. I will never be able to articulate my gratitude for the phenomenal healthcare staff I've known the graft of.

To Wayne Holloway-Smith, for your diligent mentorship; for always backing it; for having tireless faith in me, my recovery and my work. To Out-Spoken Press, for your trust and encouragement with this collection.

To Rees Greenman, who 'bit off huge chunks of life and chewed them for all their worth'; who taught me apricots are worth the stomach-ache. Rest easy, Sweetpea.

Other titles by Out-Spoken Press